SPRINGSTEEN

**TEXT BY
ROBERT HILBURN**

**ART DIRECTION BY
HOWARD KLEIN**

A ROLLING STONE PRESS BOOK
CHARLES SCRIBNER'S SONS NEW YORK

Library of Congress Cataloging in Publication Data

Hilburn, Robert.
    Springsteen.
    1. Springsteen, Bruce.   2. Rock musicians—United
States—Biography.   I. Title.
ML420.S77H4 1985   784.5′4′00924 [B]   85-14195
ISBN 0-684-18456-7
        0-684-18703-5 (pbk)

First Paperback Edition 1986

Printed in the United States of America.

Photo editor: Amanda Joy Rubin

Jacket photographs by Jeffrey Mayer (front)
and Neal Preston/Camera 5 (back)

SPRINGSTEEN

SPRINGSTEEN

ACKNOWLEDGMENTS

•

ROBERT HILBURN WOULD LIKE TO THANK: TIM McGINNIS, A SENSITIVE AND ASTUTE EDITOR WHO REALLY LISTENS TO THE MUSIC; CHRISTOPHER CONNELLY, WHOSE SUGGESTIONS PROVIDED SOME SPIRIT IN THE NIGHT TO PARTS OF THE MANUSCRIPT; THOSE WHOSE FRIENDSHIP IS SURELY A COMFORT TO SPRINGSTEEN: JON LANDAU, STEVE VAN ZANDT, PETER PHILBIN, JIMMY IOVINE, DAVE MARSH, BARBARA CARR, AND THOSE WHOSE SUPPORT IS A BLESSING TO ME: KATHI BARR AND A SLEW OF HILBURNS: ROB, KATHY, MONTGOMERY, JOHN AND ALICE MARIE. ALSO: BRUCE SPRINGSTEEN, FOR TAKING TIME—ONCE AGAIN.

THE EDITORS OF ROLLING STONE PRESS ARE GRATEFUL FOR THE CONTRIBUTIONS OF HOWARD KLEIN, MICHAEL PIETSCH, FRANK SPOTNITZ, DEBORAH MITCHELL, MARY ASTADOURIAN, AMANDA RUBIN, SANDRA HIGASHI, HOWARD B. LIEBOWITZ, CHRISTOPHER CONNELLY AND *BACKSTREETS* MAGAZINE.

•

THE **Bottom Line**

ALLAN PEPPER & STANLEY SNADOWSKY

15 WEST FOURTH STREET, NEW YORK, NEW YORK 10012

$5.00

August 17 , 1975

AN EVENING

BRUCE SPRI

& THE E STR

Creative reigns in rock & roll are notoriously brief. Elvis Presley's most influential records were all made in the three years that ended with the release of "Jailhouse Rock" in 1956. Though he continued to exercise his questioning spirit, Bob Dylan never regained his hold on the rock audience after his motorcycle accident of 1966. The Beatles burned out before the start of the 1970s.

A decade after he was featured on the covers of *Time* and *Newsweek* in 1975, Bruce Springsteen was still reaching for his artistic and commercial peak. The most acclaimed figure in American rock by the time his album *The River* was released in 1980, Springsteen has added to both his art and his audience with his two subsequent LPs. *Nebraska*, a stark, compassionate look at loss of hope in America, dazzled critics and listeners in 1982. In 1984 *Born in the U.S.A.* spread Springsteen's hard-times portraits and personal celebrations to a huge new audience.

By the time he and the E Street Band reached Greensboro, North Carolina, in January 1985, Springsteen was halfway through an international tour that would be seen by an estimated four million people. *Born in the U.S.A.* had sold five million copies—almost double his previous high with *Born to Run*—and had just regained the Number One position on the national sales charts.

It was Springsteen's first local appearance in four years, and tickets for both shows at the 15,500-seat Greensboro Coliseum had sold out as fast as the box office could collect the money. Fans draped welcoming banners over the balcony rails ("Ooh, ooh, we gotta crush on you") and shouted his name after almost every song.

For more than three hours, Springsteen performed with an intensity that challenged both his stamina and the audience's ability to absorb. Rather than the narrow range offered in most pop music performances, Springsteen's embraced many styles and emotions—from the youthful exhilaration of his *Born to Run* days to the darker social realism of his recent work.

His fans have always been thrilled by Springsteen's energy and drive, and the Greensboro concert was no exception. But now what they seem to treasure most is his emotional honesty and integrity.

"You can't live on what you did yesterday or what's going to happen tomorrow," he told me in 1980. "If you fall into that trap, you don't belong on stage. That's what rock & roll is: a promise, an oath. It's about being as true as you can at any particular moment."

Springsteen's biggest triumph is that he has lived up to his own oath. In an age that has taught us to expect corruption and compromise, he invites trust. He has made it possible once again to put faith in a rock & roll singer.

It's dangerous to attribute anything as complex as Springsteen's motivation to a single incident or person, but there's reason to believe that much of what makes Springsteen run is based on his perception of his own first and greatest hero, Elvis Presley. After his split with Mike Appel, the aggressive ex-Marine who had managed his career for the four years climaxed by the release of *Born to Run,* Springsteen addressed the dangers of fame in these terms: "Mike Appel thought he would be Colonel Parker and I'd be Elvis. Only he wasn't Colonel Parker and I wasn't Elvis."

Elvis played an important part in the conversation the first time I met Springsteen, in 1974. Though he had built a reputation around his native New Jersey, Springsteen was largely unknown on the West Coast at the time of the interview. He and the E Street Band weren't even headliners yet. They had opened that night at the Santa Monica Civic Auditorium for Dr. John, the growly-voiced rock & blues piano player from New Orleans. But you could see that things were beginning to change for Springsteen, and he was trying to figure out how to adjust. His two Columbia albums were critically acclaimed, and his record company was promoting him aggressively.

On this evening, he was uncomfortable talking about himself. The only time he relaxed was when he spoke about Elvis.

"Before rock & roll, I didn't have any purpose. I tried to play football and baseball and all those things...and I just didn't fit. I was running through a maze. It was never a hobby. It was a reason to live. It was the only one I had. It was kind of life or death."

Bruce was eight years old when he saw Elvis on the *Ed Sullivan Show* in 1957, and Elvis became a symbol of freedom and future to a youngster from a New Jersey town that seemed a storage house for compromise and failure. When he saw Elvis, Bruce decided that's what he would be when he grew up.

In the Greensboro Coliseum in 1985, Springsteen was still talking about Elvis. Only this time his tone was different. Early in the concert, he told about driving by Graceland in 1976. Springsteen laughed as he recalled how he climbed the wall and raced to Elvis' front door, hoping to get a chance to meet him. He was caught and turned away by the guards with no sight of Elvis.

He then described his feelings when he learned that Elvis had died. "It was hard to understand how somebody whose music took away so many people's loneliness could have ended up as lonely as he did." Springsteen began singing "Bye, Bye Johnny," a song he wrote shortly after Presley's death. It's a mournful tune that ends, "You didn't have to die, you didn't have to die."

Presley's death in some ways made an even stronger impression on Springsteen than the rock star's music had. Elvis' decline was a warning and a challenge. If the young Elvis was a compelling symbol of the possible, the older Elvis was a sign of the tragedy that could accompany the realization of your dreams.

This posed some questions for Bruce: What if you remained true to the rock & roll ideal? How far could you take it? Was it possible to avoid the indifference and indulgence that eventually sabotaged the artistic vision of so many other rock heroes?

When he returned later for an encore, Springsteen performed a tender, acoustic version of "Can't Help Falling in Love," one of Elvis' trademark ballads. Springsteen's voice doesn't have the purity of Presley's but there was a touching sweetness in his rendition. Before the applause died, the rest of the E Street Band moved into place, and Springsteen tore into the most rousing version of "Born to Run" I've heard in the dozens of times I've seen him perform. The song is Springsteen's greatest expression of determination and hope. But on this night, it seemed to have an undercurrent of rage, as if Springsteen were reminding himself and everyone present that what happened to Elvis wasn't inevitable.

In the dressing room after the Greensboro concert, Springsteen reflected on maintaining balance in a field littered with failures.

"The casualty rate in this business is real high," he acknowledged. "But life is a struggle for most people. It's a thin line between surviving and not making it. It's like people with their finger in the dike, trying to hold back the flood all the time. That's what our band is about.

"The shows aren't a casual thing, even though they are filled with fun and wildness. There should be beauty, but there's also got to be ugliness and brutality. If you don't have all of that in the evening, you're not doing it. If you turn away, that's the beginning of the end. That's what you spend your time doing—trying not to turn away."

1

Childhood is a time of immense hopes and insecurities, and the neighborhoods of your childhood chronicle those emotions better than a diary. Old street corners and playgrounds remind you of early aspirations and doubts, setbacks and successes. John Lennon said he felt psychologically naked when he went back to Liverpool or bumped into one of the old gang. "That's one time when you can't hide from yourself. The records, the fame—none of it shields you. You remember exactly who you are deep inside."

Maybe that's why Bruce Springsteen finds it hard to shake a sentimental attachment to his home town—even though he spent much of his New Jersey school days yearning to get away from places like Asbury Park and Freehold. Familiar streets and faces provide an emotional anchor that can be a useful balance against the pressures of the pop spotlight, and Springsteen values that protective balance.

"One of the things that was always on my mind to do was to maintain connections with the people I'd grown up with, and the sense of the community where I came from," he said shortly after the start of the Born in the U.S.A. tour. "That's why I stayed in New Jersey. The danger of fame is in forgetting or being distracted."

Someone who has worked closely with Springsteen for years told me, "There's always part of him back home. He needs to go back there and check up on himself. I remember one night he drove me all through that area for three hours. He'd point out places and tell me some little story about something that happened there."

Most people think of Asbury Park, the seedy beachfront town on the Jersey shore, as Springsteen's home town. His debut album was called *Greetings from Asbury Park, N.J.*, and he often tells stories on stage about the years he spent there, playing clubs and trying to put his rock & roll dreams in place. But Bruce was born eighteen miles away in Freehold, New Jersey. Both of these Central Jersey towns—about an hour's drive from Manhattan or Philadelphia—take pride in their past. Asbury Park was once a thriving resort with luxury hotels and a busy boardwalk. Freehold was the site of an important battle during the Revolutionary War; there's still a museum in town with artifacts from the battle.

There's not as much to say about these towns' futures. You can picture a young Bruce walking along Main Street and out on Highway 9, ducking into the sandwich shop here and the dime store there, daydreaming about the escape that he would eventually glamorize in "Thunder Road" and "Born to Run." But the thing that strikes you about this area now is the emptiness. Walking through Freehold is like walking through any of a hundred American towns that have been strangled by changing times.

Asbury Park is more depressing than Freehold. You don't have to go to the edges of this town to find the darkness. The boardwalk—the heart of Asbury Park—was all but deserted during the two days I spent there in the summer of 1984. That day, the only sounds in the once-proud convention center were electronic zaps from a lone

"All my houses seem to have been way stations." Overleaf: The Asbury Park boardwalk, still waiting for news of the "recovery."

video game. A boy and his dog had the entire beach to themselves. Most of the attractions that lured people to Asbury Park were destroyed in a race riot more than a decade ago. There's talk about a redevelopment project to save the town, but the smart money is headed south to Atlantic City and all the new casinos.

•

THEY'RE CLOSING DOWN THE TEXTILE MILL ACROSS FROM THE RAILROAD TRACKS. FOREMAN SAYS THESE JOBS ARE GOING BOYS AND THEY AIN'T COMING BACK.
"MY HOMETOWN"

•

A few blocks away from the boardwalk, John Eddie, a young rocker who was causing a stir in the region that summer, was setting up his equipment at the Stone Pony, a club Springsteen frequently visits when he's in town.

"I think this whole area's lucky to have Bruce, especially the young people. They need something to look up to. You can see this town is beat."

"It's strange. Go a few miles one way and you've got millionaires

Below: St. Rose of Lima in Freehold, N.J. where Springsteen attended grade school. He was hard pressed to remember any good times. Right: Public high school. The yearbook tag for the self-described loner was "Bruce." Overleaf: The house on South Street where Springsteen spent most of his childhood.

walking along the boardwalk. Go a few miles the other way and you've got beautiful homes, but this place is something else. You get the feeling that the life has been sucked out of Asbury Park. It's like something from a horror novel."

Things seem more pleasant on the surface in Freehold, the county seat of Monmouth County. There's a small-town calmness that turns out, once you've been there a while, to be simply uneventfulness. Many of the young people of Freehold sense the emptiness and leave as soon as they get out of school, but a core of residents hang on. It's as if the old people in the borough have lived there so long that they don't know what they'd do somewhere else.

"I come from an area where there was not a lot of success," Springsteen once said. "I didn't know anyone who made a record before me. I didn't know anybody who had made anything."

He also said, "It was a real classic little town, very intent on maintaining the status quo. Everything was looked at as a threat. Kids were looked at as a nuisance and a threat."

One of the few things that Freehold has to speak proudly of is Springsteen. When I visited Liverpool in 1983, I found a lot of resentment toward the Beatles from people who never forgave them for moving to London after they became successful. But Freehold—and all of Jersey—is full of affection for Springsteen. One reason is that Bruce still lives in the area, even if it is in a million dollar home twenty minutes away in Rumson. They're also proud that Springsteen fans from around the world travel to Freehold and Asbury Park the way Beatles fans visit Liverpool and Elvis fans make pilgrimages to Memphis.

The Stone Pony is where most of the fans end up. Near a bar at the rear of the club, there's a collage of photos: Springsteen huddles with fans in one series, plays softball in another.

"People come here from all over the country hoping to see Bruce," explained the Stone Pony's manager, Butch Pielka. "If he's not here that night, they just take pictures of the club or something. It's not like there's a Springsteen museum. So this is the only place they know to go."

Springsteen is such an inspiration to young people throughout the state that bills were entered in the state legislature nominating "Born to Run" as the official state song.

What a great move. Too great, in fact, not to botch up. The bills were voted down. In what New Jersey textbooks may eventually describe as the great Springsteen compromise, the lawmakers finally agreed to declare "Born to Run" the state's "unofficial youth song." Some assemblymen argued that the song's lyrics set a bad example, that all the references to running away encouraged young people to flee the realities of life. In his own defense, Springsteen told *Musician* magazine in 1984, "To me, there was an aspect of [escape], but I always felt it was more about searching."

Bruce Frederick Springsteen was born on September 23, 1949, the first of three children for Douglas and Adele Springsteen. The family name is Dutch, but there's Irish blood on his father's side and

The old Freehold neighborhood—"Liverpool" for Springsteen fans.

his mother's family is Italian.

See Bruce's parents at one of his concerts and you can pick up immediately on the differences in personality. His dad is short and squat, and he looks a bit too intimidating for anyone to walk up and say hello to. Part of it is that he's shy, but there is also the reserve of a headstrong man who felt cheated for so long by life that he now finds it hard, even with his son's success, to open up.

Adele, however, jumps about like a cheerleader at the start of every song, hugging fans who stop by to say hello. She has maintained a scrapbook on Bruce ever since the days of Steel Mill, one of his first bands. Shortly after I wrote a review of *Born to Run* in 1975, I received a letter from Mrs. Springsteen:

> My husband and I want to thank you very much for the article on Bruce. Naturally, we are keeping a scrapbook and all goes in, good and bad . . . All the publicity Bruce has been getting is unbelievable, especially the cover stories on *Time* and *Newsweek*. We are very proud of him and know he can handle it all. We went to see Bruce play in Oakland and it was a night we will always remember. Bill Graham had undershirts with the cover picture of *Time* and *Newsweek* (*Time* on the front, *Newsweek* on the back).

Douglas and Adele, who met each other in Freehold, were married in 1948 and lived briefly in an apartment before moving in with Douglas's parents. That house—where Bruce was born—was torn down years ago and the land is now covered by a church parking lot. Bruce's father had various jobs, including stints as a factory worker and a prison guard. But mostly he drove a bus. Adele worked as a secretary for a land title company. The family lived briefly in a house on Institute Street that is shown on the lyric sheet for *Born in the U.S.A.*, in a photo of Springsteen leaning against a tree in the front yard. The main Springsteen residence was one side of a two-story, two-family house next to Ducky Slattery's Sinclair Station on South Street.

The house was just a couple of blocks from Freehold's downtown area and close to St. Rose of Lima, the parochial school that Bruce attended. He later went to Freehold Regional High School and took a few classes at Ocean County Community College, where he was encouraged to be a writer. But Springsteen had made up his mind early that he wanted to be a musician.

Bruce can even point to the night he made the decision. He was so excited in 1957 when he saw Elvis on the *Ed Sullivan Show* that he asked his mother for a guitar. She got him one, but also made him take lessons, which he hated so much that he put the guitar away. It wasn't until the Beatles arrived in 1964 that he tried the guitar again, buying one in a pawn shop for $18. The hours he spent in his room, listening to records and learning to play, were a constant source of tension between Bruce and his father, who wanted to see him pursue a more practical career.

By most accounts Bruce was a loner—not a flashy rebel, but still rigidly independent. Diane Forman, a high school classmate of

Steel Mill's guitar hero with regulation 1969 hair length.

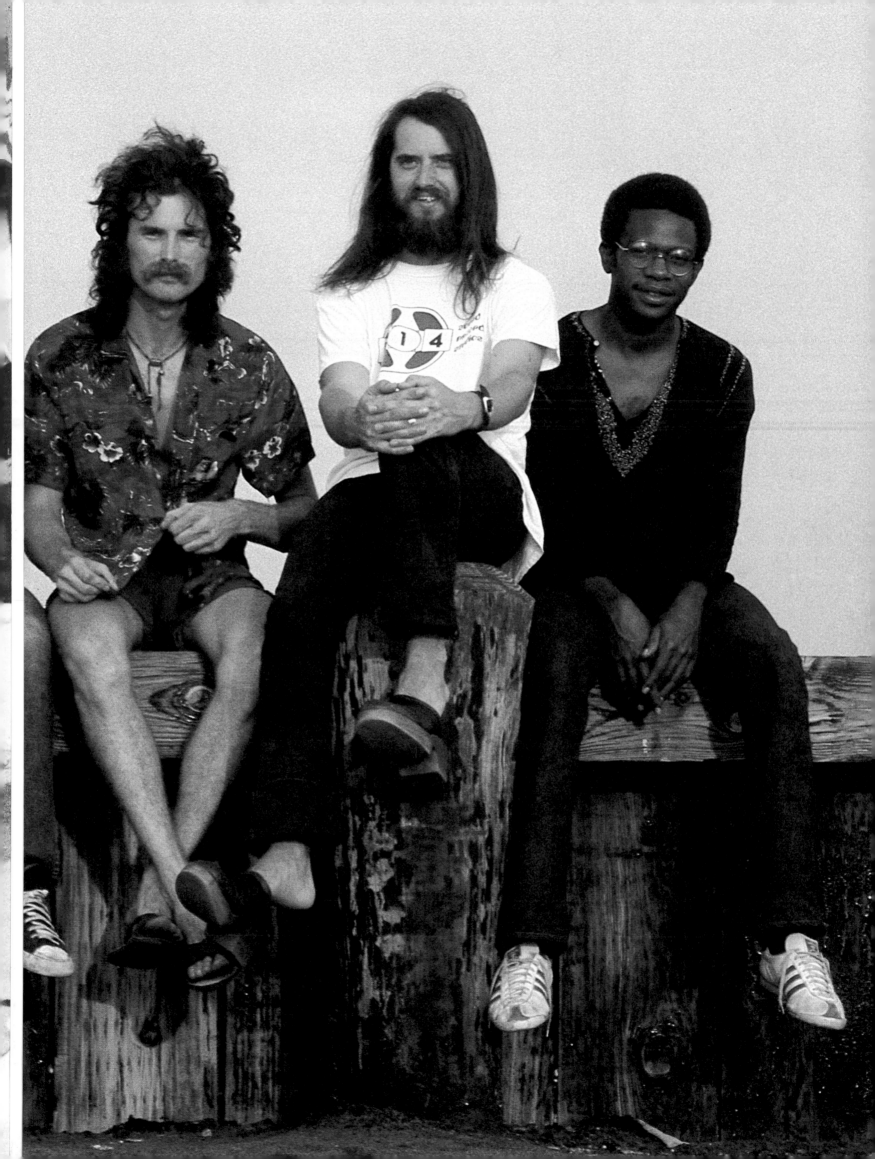

1971 devastated the boardwalk area. Springsteen would eventually be reunited with many of the musicians he worked with that year: Van Zandt, keyboardist David Sancious, saxophonist Clarence Clemons, bassist Garry Tallent. But after the Bruce Springsteen Band folded he tried it on his own for a while.

While the other musicians took day jobs to supplement their incomes, Springsteen continued to devote all his time to music. Trying every possible door, he auditioned for Mike Appel and Jim Cretecos, a minor level songwriting-production team whose major credit was writing one hit, "Don't You Want to Be Wanted," for teenybop faves the Partridge Family.

"I never got into being discouraged because I never got into hoping," Springsteen told me about this period. "When I was a kid, I never got used to expecting success. I got used to failing.

"Once you do that, the rest is real easy. It took a lot of the pressure off. I just said, 'Hell, I'm a loser. I don't have to worry about anything.' I assumed immediately that nothing was happening.

Southside Johnny Lyon (striped scarf) and the Asbury Jukes. Right, Bruce and Clarence, aka "The Big Man."

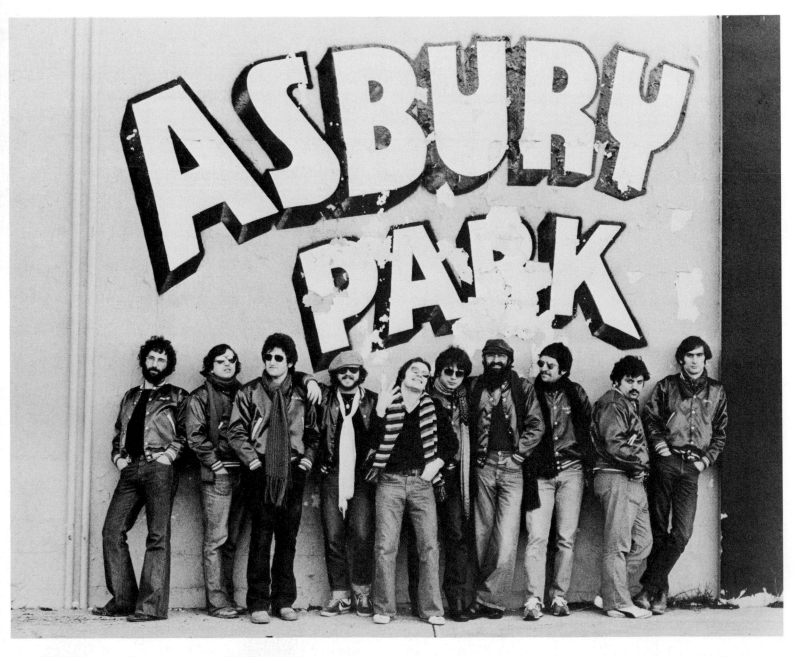

"But that's not the same as giving up. You keep trying, but you don't count on things. It can be a strength. Because I know some people who sweat out winning so much it kills them. So, in the end, they lose anyway. They win, but they lose. People don't realize things can often be just the opposite of what they seem."

Appel and Cretecos agreed to manage Springsteen early in 1972. The contract—signed at night on the hood of a car—would come to haunt Springsteen. At the time, however, Springsteen was busy writing songs "like a madman" as he has said often. "Had no money, nowhere to go, nothing to do. Didn't know too many people. It was cold and I wrote a lot. And I got to feeling very guilty if I didn't."

On May 3, Appel arranged for an audition with John Hammond, the CBS executive who had signed Bob Dylan a decade before. In *Born to Run,* Dave Marsh relates what happened when the cocky Appel first met Hammond. "You're the guy who discovered Bob Dylan, huh? Well, we want to find out if that was just luck or if you really have ears."

What a guy. It's not hard to see how Springsteen and Appel would clash eventually.

But that day in 1972, Springsteen nervously walked into the CBS office with Appel, sat at the piano and played almost a dozen songs, five of which showed up on his first album: "Growin' Up," "It's Hard to Be a Saint in the City," "Mary Queen of Arkansas," "Does This Bus Stop at 82nd Street?" and "The Angel." Hammond was excited by the imagination and dazzle of the words. Springsteen walked out of the room with a future.

•

I WAS OPEN TO THE PAIN AND CROSSED BY
   THE RAIN AND I WALKED ON A CROOKED
   CRUTCH
I STROLLED ALL ALONE THROUGH A
   FALLOUT ZONE AND CAME OUT WITH MY
   SOUL UNTOUCHED
I HID IN THE CLOUDED WRATH OF THE
   CROWN, BUT WHEN THEY SAID "SIT DOWN,"
   I STOOD UP—
OOOH...GROWIN' UP

•

As soon as the deal with Columbia Records was complete, Springsteen began gathering up the old gang—Clemons, Lopez, Tallent, Federici and Sancious—to make the record. The only trouble was that Hammond saw Springsteen as a folk-style singer-songwriter, not as a rock & roller. Like Mike Appel initially, Hammond didn't want anything to interfere with Springsteen's words.

The album, *Greetings from Asbury Park, N.J.*, was a compromise between Hammond's preference for folk and Springsteen's rock

Mike Appel, the man who moved moguls for Springsteen. He got the face-to-face interview with John Hammond of Columbia.

instincts. It was recorded in just three weeks and co-produced by Appel and Cretecos for Laurel Canyon Ltd., their publishing and production company.

Because of the folk emphasis, the LP seemed primarily a showcase for Springsteen's words. He was already dealing with the issues of integrity and responsibility that would be at the heart of his best work, but he hadn't developed much clarity as a writer. The influences of Dylan and Van Morrison ricochet through many of the songs, and some of the album's images are clumsy, even almost incomprehensible. Still, there was an enormous excitement and promise in the outpouring of images and rhymes, encompassing everything from Catholic school memories to Springsteen's relentless drive. The album overflowed with the sheer exhilaration of someone testing his creative prowess.

Springsteen's sound hadn't jelled yet either. His arrangements owed heavily to the soul and R&B stylings of Van Morrison, particularly the keyboard and horn sounds. The steady back beat suggests the famed Motown rhythm section, and the horn arrangements echo the Memphis Stax sound. It's big city music with smooth sax lines and handclaps over Bruce's miked acoustic guitar. He would almost talk his lyrics over David Sancious' spare, jazzy

Preceding page: Enter Miami Steve Van Zandt and Max Weinberg. Below: The first E Street band. Early on, the albums were playing characters and setting off each other.

"Everybody has it but most people just never figure it out," Springsteen once explained, talking about talent and potential. "You've got to be able to see yourself for what you are, and not until then can you be what you want to be."

In the weeks after the release of *Greetings from Asbury Park, N.J.* Springsteen was busy figuring out who he was. He was proud of the first album, but he knew that it was just a beginning—more an exercise in creative energy than a definition of his own vision.

His second album was released in November 1973, and went a long way toward codifying Springsteen's artistic identity. His first album may have had an Asbury Park postcard on its cover, but it was wildly jumbled in its locations and themes, as if his mind were so filled with images and emotions that he could hardly pin them down to a specific place. *The Wild, The Innocent and the E Street Shuffle* became his statement of roots.

The music celebrates a catalogue of American music styles: the churchy organ and carnival calliope sounds (reminiscent of Garth Hudson and Richard Manuel's keyboard interplay in the Band), the funky wah-wah over the lead guitar on "E Street Shuffle," the folk guitar and harmonica, the marching band tempos, the horns fat and mournful. Ariel Swartley picked this album as her desert island companion in Greil Marcus' anthology, *Stranded*, observing that Springsteen treats rock as "our common language, our shared mythology." We recognize the Spector echo, the James Brown funk sound and the "Dion-ysian brawls." Springsteen "triggers memories like you were a jukebox and he was the man with all the quarters." The band stretches out here, and their music is joyous, full of the soul choruses of the big ensemble groups that played Asbury Park's boardwalk roadhouses.

"I don't know what I'm writing from, but the main thing I've always been worried about was me," he explained. "I had to write about me all the time, every song, 'cause in a way, you're trying to find out what that 'me' is. That's why I chose where I grew up, and where I live, and I take situations I'm in, and people I know, and take them to the limits."

Sure there was good-time, Gary U.S. Bonds-style rock & roll—witness the frat-rock "everybody form a line" chants of "The E Street Shuffle." But despite those bursts of party-time energy, grimmer moods were starting to emerge in his music and lyrics. His songs told stories of people trapped by their environments: searching for love and transcendence in the streets of a Jersey shore town, over the river in the big city, or on the boardwalk on the Fourth of July. There were the sentimental strains of accordions and calliopes in his songs. Balancing that melancholia, though, was an increasing sense of seasoned, hard-won optimism: that the emptiness in people's lives could be overcome with compassion and a willingness to take risks.

Springsteen's philosophy was emerging. The vagabond circus image of "Wild Billy's Circus Story" was the perfect metaphor for

Springsteen's music draws from many American music sources: Motown, Stax-Volt, Dylan, Elvis and a little garage band music, too.

what rock & roll meant to him: membership in a lively but outcast community, and the rootlessness of the road. The life Springsteen saw ahead was exciting, certainly, but also hard, often lonely. Springsteen wasn't thinking of rock & roll as a path to luxury. He was thinking truths.

The album included two songs which would become audience favorites for years to come. "Rosalita (Come out Tonight)" was a typically autobiographical effort: a witty, libidinous tale of a rock star and his girlfriend that became Bruce's best-loved song. Its sassy digressions and fun-loving knocks at parental disapproval showed Bruce assuming control over his story-telling, beginning to marshal his powers of observation into coherent, pungent frameworks.

"4th of July, Asbury Park (Sandy)" showed a more wistful side, the verses whispered as if he was singing into his girlfriend's ear. This was a Springsteen ready to acknowledge failure ("Sandy, that waitress I was seeing lost her desire for me/I spoke with her last night, she said she won't set herself on fire for me anymore"), a Springsteen looking for love but looking even more for a way out of his dead-end existence. More than "Rosalita," "4th of July" had an intimacy and an immediacy that was deeply affecting.

I had enjoyed Springsteen's first two albums, even putting the second on the 1974 year-end Ten Best list I compiled for the Los Angeles *Times*. So when I saw that he was coming through town that summer, opening for Dr. John, I called Columbia Records and asked for an interview. To my surprise, the publicist called back to say Springsteen wasn't doing any interviews. Everyone in rock & roll does interviews—except Dylan. Was this guy starting to take that "New Dylan" stuff seriously?

I didn't press the matter. Life goes on and, besides, Arista Records had been nagging me to do a profile of its new president, Clive Davis, the Sunday I was planning to write about Springsteen.

I mentioned the Davis interview to the Columbia publicist and got a surprising response. Columbia was having its national convention in Los Angeles the Sunday the Davis story would appear, and since Davis—the man who had okayed John Hammond's recommendation to sign Springsteen—had recently been ousted as president of CBS Records, the last thing the local CBS office wanted was a big spread on Davis, possibly quoting him about how much more he enjoyed life now that he was away from CBS.

After talking to her bosses at CBS, the publicist called back to ask if there wasn't some way I could run the Davis interview some other Sunday. I said sure: I'd postpone Davis a week if I could get Springsteen. The word was relayed that afternoon from CBS: deal.

I don't know what CBS did to get Bruce to do the interview, but I later learned that label executives in New York had to step in and convince Springsteen to talk. As I headed for the Santa Monica Civic Auditorium that night, I wondered what this guy Springsteen was like. Who ever would have expected the guy who wrote songs as marvelous as "Sandy" and "Rosalita" to be a prima donna?

Playing from memory: "There ain't a note I play onstage that can't be traced directly back to my mother and father."

The word sounds corny now, but there was something about Springsteen that made it seem reasonable in person. Here was someone who was onto something new. I didn't know quite what it was, but I found myself pulling for him. I had loved rock ever since the first time I saw Elvis, too, but I wasn't sure I put quite as much faith in it as Springsteen did. Rock had lost a lot of its heart in the '70s. Could he make us all believe in it again?

The Wild, the Innocent still didn't establish Springsteen as a commercial force. It, too, failed to crack the *Billboard* Top 200 list, selling only about 50,000 copies in its first year. But the LP earned Springsteen even more critical support than *Greetings*. That support may have kept Springsteen on Columbia Records, where he was on delicate ground after Clive Davis was fired in 1973.

A cadre of Springsteen supporters at Columbia continued to believe in him and they saw the glowing reviews as a sign that he could break through commercially if he just got more exposure. Radio airplay, except in a few East Coast areas, had been almost nonexistent on the first two albums.

The most important review in Columbia's eyes appeared in the May 22 issue of Boston's *Real Paper*. It was written by Jon Landau, one of the half-dozen most important critics in the country. Besides writing for the *Real Paper,* he edited the *Rolling Stone* record review section.

"It's four in the morning and raining. I'm 27 today, feeling old, listening to my records, and remembering that things were different a decade ago. In 1964, I was a freshman at Brandeis University, playing guitar and banjo five hours a day, listening to records most of the rest of the time, jamming with friends during the late-night hours, working out the harmonies to Beach Boys' and Beatles' songs."

Describing a loss of enthusiasm he had felt as he became more involved with the music business as a record producer and critic, Landau continued.

"Today I listen to music with a certain measure of detachment. I'm a professional and I make my living commenting on it. There are months when I love my work and months when I hate it, going through the routine just as a shoe salesman goes through his.

"But tonight there is someone I can write of the way I used to write, without reservations of any kind. Last Thursday, at the Harvard Square theater, I saw my rock 'n' roll past flash before my eyes. And I saw something else: I saw rock 'n' roll future and its name is Bruce Springsteen. And on a night when I needed to feel young, he made me feel like I was hearing music for the very first time."

Columbia Records made "rock 'n' roll future" the cornerstone of a massive campaign.

Springsteen was on such shaky ground at CBS in the months after *The Wild, the Innocent* that the label asked him to do what amounts to a test recording before they allowed him to proceed with the third album. He went into the studio and cut the song "Born to Run." In retrospect it's easy to think that anyone could see that "Born to Run" was a classic rock & roll track. But no one cheered as Bruce walked out of the studio. This rendition of "Born to Run" was

Springsteen and the old E Street band bed down in Cambridge, Mass., 1973 with Joe Spadafora (white socks), the owner of Joe's Place.

muddy, heightening suspicions around the company that Springsteen just couldn't make a commercial record. The track also cost $10,000, considered an outrageous amount at the time. Alarmed executives wondered what the whole album would cost.

Besides, CBS thought Bruce had an attitude problem. The label had worked hard on a plan to get Springsteen exposure. They helped him get the opening slot on a national tour by Chicago, one of Columbia's biggest acts. But Bruce quit the tour after only about a dozen shows. He felt he couldn't capture all the emotional aspects of his music in the thirty or forty-five minutes that was allotted to him as an opening act. He declared that in the future he would appear only as a headliner.

The reaction at CBS was that he must be crazy. He took too much time between records, his lyrics were too long, his vocals were hard to understand, he wouldn't show up at radio stations for promotions, and he didn't even want to do interviews.

Bruce just didn't think any of that was his concern. His business was music. It was Mike Appel's job to stand between Bruce and the company. And the abrasive way Appel passed that message to Columbia was another mark against Springsteen.

But the reviews helped and so did the enthusiasm of people like publicists Ron Oberman and Peter Philbin and promotion director Mike Pillot. Springsteen and Appel went back into the studio and remixed "Born to Run."

During the months before the release of *Born to Run*, Springsteen became involved in a growing partnership with Jon Landau. The critic moved to New York, for reasons that had nothing to do with Springsteen, and began attending some of the *Born to Run* album sessions. Springsteen had been bogged down in the project. He was having trouble getting the wide-screen sounds in his head onto record. Landau offered helpful perspective. By March 1975, Landau was officially listed as co-producer.

According to everyone involved, the sessions were grueling. Springsteen knew he was onto a breakthrough and he refused to compromise.

"I was unsure about the album all the way," he explained shortly after it was released. "I didn't really know what I put down on it. I lost all perspective...the [sessions] turned into something I never conceived of a record turning into. It turned into this thing that was wrecking me, just pounding me into the ground. Every time you'd win a little victory over it, accomplish a little something you'd say, 'Well, the worst is over.' The next day you'd come back in and it would start pounding away at you again."

Landau, coming into the project fresh, helped Springsteen edit some songs and tighten arrangements. Of Springsteen's tireless insistence on looking at every song from every angle, someone close to Springsteen once said, "The indecision comes from fear. If you do one thing, that means you can't do another. Bruce wants it all. He always wants it all."

All business: Springsteen, Clemons and Frederici.

*Born to Run* breathed with the same kind of discovery that made Elvis Presley's *Sun Sessions* and Bob Dylan's *Highway 61 Revisited* the two most important American rock albums before it. Listening to all three works, you feel present at the forging of a major artistic vision. You sense the artist's excitement at finding something within himself that he hadn't known was there until it burst forth in the studio.

While *Sun Sessions*, Presley's first recordings, unveiled rock & roll as we now define it, and *Highway 61 Revisited* updated the energy and drive of early rock and added a fierce intelligence, *Born to Run* demonstrated that Springsteen had the instincts, ambition and knowledge of rock's history to put the pieces of the fragmented rock scene back together. It was the purest glimpse in nearly a decade of the passion and power that had once been rock's hallmarks.

First there was "Thunder Road." An earlier generation had seen the elements of their romantic dreams symbolized by Fred Astaire and Ginger Rogers in the "Night and Day" sequence of *The Gay Divorcee*: an elegant ballroom, two glasses of champagne and a cheek-to-cheek dance. "Thunder Road" defined and celebrated a different dream of romance for a new generation: a car, a stretch of road and "one last chance to make it real."

Early demos reveal that while the song's pining, urgent melody took shape over time, its stunning lyrics were there from the beginning. Springsteen's images in "Thunder Road" are as immediate as Chuck Berry's and as haunting as Dylan's: Mary dancing alone on the porch, in her bed yearning for her lost loves, her boyfriends crying out her name into the nighttime air. It's a sad portrait that's redeemed by one last hope: "Tonight we will be free/All the promises will be broken," he cries, climaxing this tale of passionate love and personal transcendence that moves me as much today as it did when I first heard it.

But lyrics were only one part of Springsteen's design. Springsteen was as concerned with the sound of the record. The music was fiery, sensual and intense. Springsteen was nowhere near the pure singer Presley was, but he is arrestingly effective in the gritty, vernacular manner of Dylan.

The music itself is best represented by the album's title track, as triumphant a synthesis as we're likely to hear of everything that has been important in American rock & roll. What Phil Spector did for maximum sound at one take with wall of sound hits like "Then He Kissed Me," "Uptown" and "Baby I Love You," is what Springsteen, Appel and Landau produced—in their own version—for the '70s. If the drums, cymbals, piano and organ don't cover the audio spectrum, the guitars, voices and saxes surely will. *Born to Run* is lush. It's one big meal of a record. Vini Lopez and David Sancious had left the band, and their drum and piano spots were taken by Max Weinberg and Roy Bittan respectively. Weinberg played drums like his idols Levon Helm of the Band (Max even covers his snare with heavy paper towels to get that flat, wooden Memphis blues drum sound) and Ringo Starr, the king of the immovable, rock solid backbeat. Bittan's piano playing is strong and versatile. He is com-

fortable in many styles and serves as the transitional player during the live shows. Danny Federici's organ swirls in the mix and he wields his famed electric glockenspiel with inspired abandon. Its romantic, evocatory chiming coupled with Springsteen and Van Zandt's majestic guitar lines make "Born to Run" sound like Roy Orbison leading the world's funkiest halftime marching band.

Springsteen sings much more effectively on "Born to Run," and he's never sounded more confident. He shouts, growls and catches his voice like Elvis and Orbison did when they sang on the Sun label. Clarence solos like King Curtis, Bittan is funky, and bassist Gary Tallent and Weinberg click immediately. Springsteen stitched these elements together with an urgent, anthemic edge that made the record seem the work of an obsessed artist who feared he might never get another chance in the studio—or the passion of someone touched by a vision.

Make no mistake: *Born to Run* wasn't a flawless album. Just as Springsteen leaned too heavily on influences like Dylan, Van Morrison and the Band in his first album, the sources of some of the ideas on "Born to Run" lie too near the surface, from the Phil Spector-style orchestration of many of the songs to the Dylanesque organ introduction to "Backstreets." Still, the album's best selections are revelations of the highest order in rock.

Springsteen has often said that he felt reborn the night he wrote "Born to Run," and his thrill and confidence spilled over to the E Street Band's recording of the cut and the live shows.

It's no accident that the members of the band nicknamed Springsteen "the Boss." He doesn't dominate absolutely—there is room for group members to express themselves—but his word is final, though all band shares of the concert take are equal (to new guy Nils Lofgren's amazement). Bruce will get incensed if an E Streeter misses a song cue. When he brings his arm down, Max Weinberg hits the drum. What he wants on the record goes on the record. Bruce doesn't have to threaten, but he has his rules: no drugs, be on time, be on the bus when it leaves. Though the band's personnel was stable from the time of *Born to Run* up to the Born in the U.S.A. tour, there were some changes required earlier. Vini Lopez, the drummer, occasionally would speed up the beat on stage, and, according to a longtime associate of Springsteen's, Bruce was probably not too disappointed when Lopez left the band. Ernest "Boom" Carter replaced him. David Sancious is an outstanding pianist and Bruce admired his technical ability. But Sancious and Springsteen's musical ideas began to diverge. Perhaps, the associate has noted, his long, fluid solos seemed out of place in the band's arrangements. David's parting with the E Street Band was amicable and he left to make his own albums, taking Lopez's replacement, Carter, with him.

Preceding page: Bruce and Miami Steve play The Carlton Theater in Red Bank, New Jersey, October, 1975. Left, After a grueling summer in the studio making *Born to Run,* Springsteen had every reason to sound exultant in concert. "Born to Run" was a hit single (at four and a half minutes long) and this was his first national tour.

expectations, it caused a backlash among those who feel the need to resist anything that's sold too hard. Discovery is part of the rock experience, and all the press attention had taken that possibility away from the fans.

Springsteen wasn't enthralled with the idea of the covers. Appel had to browbeat him into doing the interviews, inviting the *Time* reporter, for instance, on an airplane flight with them and then making sure that the reporter was seated next to Bruce. Even when the magazines came out, Springsteen tried to ignore them. But Steve Van Zandt bought dozens of copies of each and plastered them all over Bruce's room.

It would have been safer for Springsteen to have his career progress gradually but steadily from the first album through the Top 10 success of *Born to Run*. But pop artists cannot choose their own ground rules or conditions. The fact is Springsteen's career did not progress steadily. His first two records received virtually no airplay and he couldn't get concert bookings in most parts of the country. Even with all the attention and sales, *Born to Run* still wasn't being played on many major Top 40 stations.

The future might have been tougher for Springsteen because of the way he had come to the public's attention, but there might not have been a future without all the exposure. Springsteen finally had an audience. His future would depend on how well he reacted to the pressures and challenges. The important thing, in the end, would be the appeal of his music.

Ultimately, Appel was right. Springsteen was good enough to withstand the obstacles. Only Appel wasn't there to enjoy the victory.

"I haven't changed, but things around me have changed," Springsteen told me a week before the covers hit the stands. "I'm not sure what it all means yet. I haven't had time to sit down and decide what's new that's fun and what's new that's not.

"But I do wonder about it sometimes. What am I doing on the cover of *Time* and *Newsweek*? I'm not the president. I'm really just a simple guy. I got my band and my music, and I love 'em both. That's my world. My life. It always has been."

This was the first time I had seen Bruce since the Santa Monica show a year before. I had gone to his afternoon soundcheck at the Roxy in West Hollywood and was now riding back to the hotel with him and Glen Brunman, a Columbia publicist and another of the long-time supporters of Springsteen in the company.

As the car moved down Sunset Blvd., Brunman pointed out a huge *Born to Run* billboard on top of a building. I turned around and looked at it through the car's back window. Doing so, I could see Springsteen tensed in the backseat and his house-size photo on the billboard through the window. Brunman slowed down so that he, too, could see the billboard. The only person who wasn't looking was Springsteen.

Most rock stars would be thrilled at the sudden upswing in their

The hype rained down on the newsstands and the billboards, but the music was still the thing that would make or break Springsteen.

career, but Springsteen was already anxious about the changes in his life. He seemed trapped, off-stride.

Some quotes seem far more interesting in retrospect. Bruce's remarks actually defined his whole purpose. But they seemed so matter of fact at the time that I buried them in the story I wrote the next day.

Asked if all that was being written about him put added pressure on him when he went on stage, Springsteen replied, "I don't know if it makes it any harder. It has always been hard in a way. Everytime you get on stage, you have to prove something. It doesn't matter if they've heard you or not. The kid on the street will make up his own mind. The music is what really matters. That's the way it has always been."

As Brunman turned off Sunset toward the hotel, Springsteen heard the faint sounds of the Byrds' version of Dylan's "My Back Pages" on the car radio. "Turn it up," he shouted. "Turn it up." The car was already at the hotel, but Bruce didn't get out. He leaned back against the seat, closing his eyes as he listened. It was his first chance to relax in a hectic day of sound checks and photo sessions. The way he slumped against the seat told more about the hectic pace and demands made upon him than he would say.

Springsteen seemed totally refreshed, however, by the time he stepped on stage that night at the Roxy. There were slow spots in Springsteen's show; the occasional miniscenes, in which he tried to recapture the feel of a New Jersey street as an introduction to a song, weren't as natural or as affecting as they would become later.

There were also uneven moments musically. Because the *Born to Run* album was such a major advance in Springsteen's writing, the older songs—including "Spirit in the Night" and "The E Street Shuffle"—seemed to drag in comparison. In light of all the media attention, it was important to remember that Springsteen was still a growing artist.

But Springsteen was as stirring in his best moments on stage as anyone in rock. The magic of his show was that it combined entertainment and purpose. He could delight you with his antics—including dancing on the table tops—but he could also touch you deeply with songs as gloriously affirming as any in rock.

These songs from *Born to Run* told us where Springsteen was coming from and where he wanted to go. To continue growing artistically, he would have to begin examining the consequences of that journey.

Looking back on that period, Springsteen said at the start of the Born in the U.S.A. tour, "[That album] really dealt with faith and a searching for answers... I laid out a set of values. A set of ideas...intangibles like faith and hope, belief in friendship and in a better way.

"But you don't really know what those values are worth until you test them. So many things happened to me so fast... I always felt that if the music was right, I would survive. But if that went wrong, then that was the end of it."

Bruce patrolling the outfield during an E Street softball game. Baserunners respected his songwriting, but what about his arm?

5

The Born to Run tour should have [...]
of Springsteen's life, but they turned [...]
sensitive to the destructive side effect [...]
if he, too, wasn't becoming overwhe [...]
sign to lots of people and that bro [...]
prefers to say, distractions.

"There was all the publicity and a [...]
1980. "I felt the thing I wanted m [...]
swept away and I didn't know if I c [...]

"That bothered me a lot, being p[...]
passing by. I'd been playing for te[...]
from, every inch of the way. I kne[...]
wanted."

After a brief U.S. tour, Springstee[...]
Europe in November 1975 for a few[...]
two nights at the Hammersmith Od[...]
steen was beginning to attract some [...]
bestseller. CBS's London staff, eage[...]
spirit of Columbia's U.S. campai[...]
drums. Stickers were plastered all o[...]
declaring, AT LAST LONDON IS REA[...]

Springsteen, sensitive to charges [...]
uncharacteristic rage when he saw t[...]
theater, ripping them down, and—[...]
Maker—even considered canceling[...]
subdued.

About that night, he later recalle[...]
With a Zombie' routine. It was noth[...]
me. It was the inside world. It's a ha[...]
a lot about my strengths and weakne[...]
that particular night."

Mike Appel recognized the sever[...]
so mad that night in London," he e[...]
And I guess I looked just as guilty t[...]
with *Time* and *Newsweek*. He wa[...]
guess he wanted it on his own term[...]

The learning process wasn't ov[...]
Springsteen resumed touring in the[...]
lower. The night of February 15, 1[...]
in his life that he didn't want to go[...]

"At that moment, I could see how[...]
drugs, because the one thing you [...]
distracted—in a big way," he told [...]

To understand Springsteen's de[...]
look at what originally attracted hi[...]
over that rock & roll brought purp[...]
himself for the first time when he s[...]
discovered that the more he devote[...]
he felt. He saw the music as a test [...]
that his future was tied to it. His pur[...]
obsession.

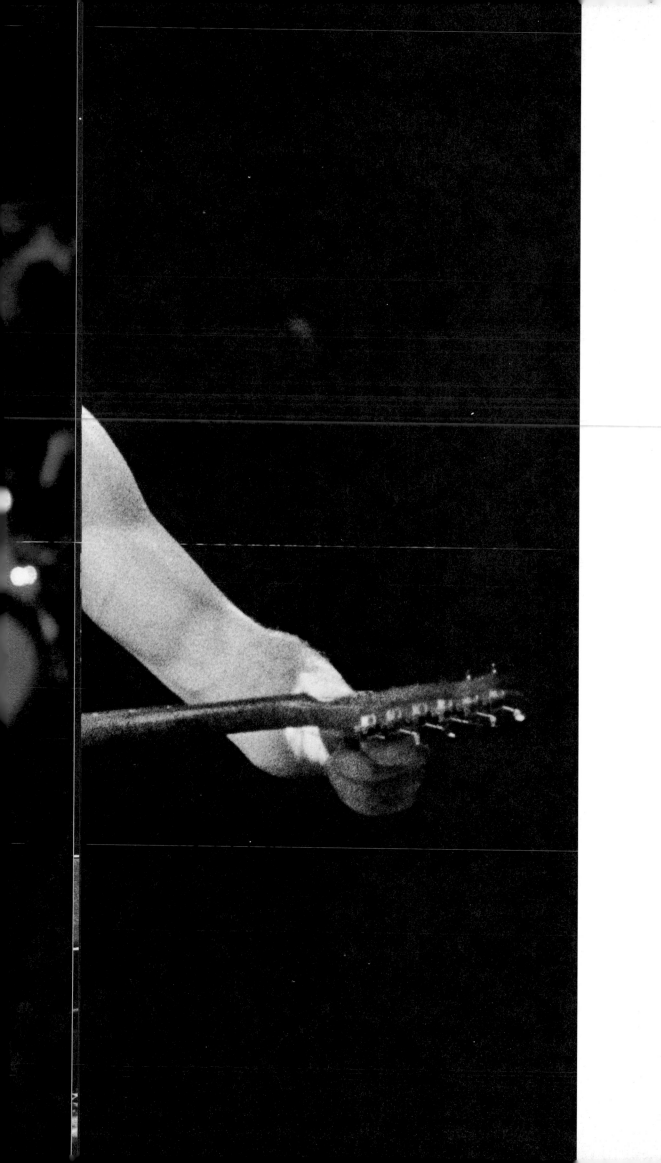

In the late spring and summer of 1981, Springsteen took his juggernaut to Europe, where he hadn't played since his ill-fated shows in 1975. By all accounts, he was received with an enthusiasm comparable to that of his stateside audiences. Offstage, though, he found that many people there thought of America as a land fueled by greed and self-interest. He started poring through books on America history—and pondered the gap between the country's ideals and its direction. His reading of Southern writers like Flannery O'Connor may have reinforced the strong sense of place and almost cinematic feel of his song lyrics.

He returned to America for a second series of shows, including the first shows of any kind at New Jersey's new venue, the 20,000-seat Brendan Byrne Arena in East Rutherford. Predictably, the home-town boy's return was greeted with particular joy, especially when he played a surprise cover, Tom Waits' "Jersey Girl." He even journeyed down to Red Bank, New Jersey, where he and the E Streeters inaugurated Clarence Clemons' club, Big Man's West, with a sweat-drenched set of oldies like "Around and Around," "You Can't Sit Down" and "Jole Blon," the song that Springsteen had sung with Gary U.S. Bonds on the latter's comeback record.

But for all Bruce's buoyancy, the arena shows had some darker underpinnings. Bruce's raps grew longer and more poignant. Perhaps confused by a newer, younger audience that knew him only from the *The River*, Springsteen started asking for quiet before his more serious songs: a solemn solo version of "This Land Is Your Land," his tribute to Elvis, "Johnny Bye Bye" (a speeded-up version of which appears on the B-side of the "I'm on Fire" single) and the unforgettable "Trapped," plucked off a Jimmy Cliff cassette Bruce dug up in Europe.

The setting was still more sobering on August 20th, when Bruce played the first of a series of shows at the Los Angeles Memorial Sports Arena. Opening night was a benefit for the Vietnam Veterans of America Foundation, and the show began not with a typical Springsteen crowd-rouser, but with a brief talk by the foundation's president, Robert Muller. As wheelchair-ridden vets lined the stage, Muller spoke of the pain of the veteran and of his joy that rock & roll could bring disparate factions together under a musical banner. The packed house listened with remarkable attentiveness.

With that as a prelude, Bruce and his band launched into a shuddering version of Creedence Clearwater Revival's "Who'll Stop the Rain," a banshee cry against governmental hypocrisy and distrust. That night he played his usual show of superb music—but he also talked to his audience perhaps more than he'd ever done before. He didn't have to ask for quiet—the mere force of his words hushed the crowds as he spoke of the agony of so many of his countrymen, cut off forever from the American Dream, people like the protagonist of "Johnny Bye Bye":

The *River* Tour ran for some 139 shows over eleven and a half months. Springsteen seasoned his last three-hour set with "Mony Mony", the Tommy James and the Shondells' hit dropped into his Mitch Ryder medley.

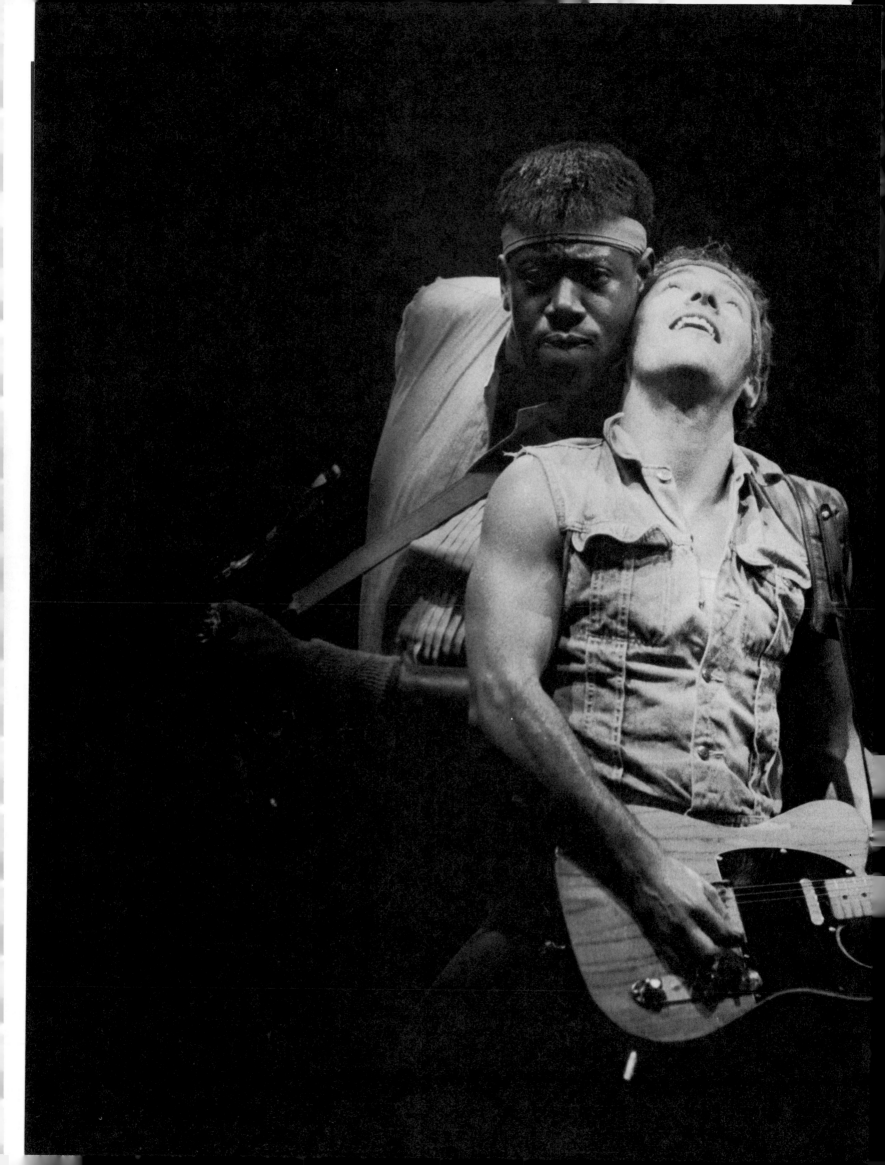

locker room. He smiled warmly, but looked tired. He didn't look like he had the strength to walk to the van that would take him to the hotel, much less return to the Coliseum the next night for another three-hour concert.

Springsteen's devotion to his craft suggests that he has a workaholic syndrome. Bruce often describes what he does as a job, perhaps a reminder of the work and dedication involved. A friend once drew an athletic metaphor in describing how Bruce approaches his art: "You've got two guys with natural talents. Bruce is the guy who respects his talent. He's always in shape, constantly in training—as opposed to the guy next to him who knows he's good and talented but doesn't mind coasting, and who counts on his innate ability a little too much, doesn't realize how much work he's got to put into it."

Some of those around Springsteen notice a loosening up, however.

"Everything about him tells me he's happier now than any time since I met him," one Springsteen ally said after the Greensboro concert. "He has so much confidence about the work he is doing right now that he is able to increase the time he spends on his personal life. It means he doesn't have to do this twenty-four hours a day any longer."

As we chatted, I thought again about the question of sacrifice, and

Left: Bruce unwinds backstage despite a security breach by costumed Kodiak bear. Below: Bussing a fan.

aunt, Dora Kirby, told me the morning after the news hit the papers. "She's a wonderful girl...just what Bruce needed."

After nearly twenty years of believing there wasn't room for anything except rock & roll in his life, Springsteen finally realized there was a place for something—or someone—else.

Springsteen had obviously thought a lot about this himself lately.

"I think you can make anything happen. That's my approach. To blame something on your job is an excuse, no matter what it is. It can make it difficult, no doubt about it. But in the end, you do what you want to do. That's what I basically believe. All the rest is excuses."

Finally, I switched the topic back to the pressures on his end, the matter of his trying to live up to what Elvis first represented to him.

He looked at me kind of skeptically. He wasn't sure about this Elvis comparison. He seemed to be squirming a bit on the stand.

"I think about Elvis a lot and what happened to him," he said finally. "The demands that this profession make on you are unreasonable. It's very strange to go out and have people look at you like you're Santa Claus or the Easter Bunny.

"It's a confusing experience for them, too. Who are they meeting? They're not quite sure. If you don't respond exactly as they imagined or something, which you're not gonna...it can be a strange experience. If you expect it to be a reasonable thing, it can drive you crazy. The answer is trying to stay healthy—mentally, physically, spiritually—all under a lot of pressure."

As an assistant signaled Bruce that the van was ready for the ride to the hotel, I raised the question again about his audience and how he has been able to avoid the isolation that surrounded Elvis. In Greensboro, as elsewhere, he seemed approachable, not a distant pop star.

"That's important because it kind of makes the whole thing more real," Bruce responded. "You want people to see that you are a human being, and you are doing your best under difficult circumstances [laughs], like everybody is. That's one of the things you want to communicate, 'Hey, it's tough, but keep going.'

"It's like giving people hope and giving yourself hope. You have to be a part of your audience in a fashion. You write the song just for yourself, but it's no good unless you play it for somebody else. That's the connection between people that is forever lasting and can never be broken apart."

Before leaving, Springsteen considered a final question. What about the faith people have in you? Is that a source of strength or is it something that drains you?

"There are times you think about those things, and there are times you don't," Bruce said. "You generally think about them when you have to, when you are confronted with a question or a decision. The rest of the time, you are like a guy just trying to do a good job.

"While you do have the responsibility to do a good job, you don't have a responsibility of carrying 20,000 people's dreams and

Preceding pages: Detroit's own Mitch Ryder, belting out "Devil with a Blue Dress On", one of his white soul hits that influenced Springsteen.

desires. That's their job.

"I do my job and they do theirs, and there is a place where you come together and support each other equally almost in your quest for the things that you want, that you need, the love you are looking for or whatever. That's what the concerts are."

When Springsteen emerged from the dressing room, a couple dozen fans and arena employees were waiting. As I've seen him do so often, he stopped to sign autographs and pose for photos. Back at the hotel, some more fans were waiting and he went through the same process again before heading to his room and sleep.

Bruce had reached another plateau. He was the most respected and possibly the most popular rock star in the world. This was the time, ironically, that he should have been on the covers of *Time* and *Newsweek*. But the world rarely works rationally.

Anyone who remembers how Springsteen labored under the "new Bob Dylan tag" in the early '70s would have been intrigued by the scene in A&M's Hollywood recording studios on January 28, 1985. More than forty American pop stars had gathered to record a song—"We Are the World"—as part of a USA for Africa project to raise funds for famine victims.

To maximize the record's appeal, organizers had invited singers representing different areas and styles. The stars ranged from Michael Jackson and Lionel Richie to Willie Nelson and Ray Charles to Bette Midler and Cyndi Lauper. In the studio, this diversity resulted in a colorful mix of hairstyles and wardrobes.

From the rear of the room, however, two artists looked exactly alike as they stepped to the microphones for their solos. Springsteen and Dylan both wore black leather jackets, black pants and heavy boots. With their dark unkempt hair, they looked like they had just tumbled out of a laundry hamper.

As they began singing their respective lines, however, the differences between these two major rock figures seemed far stronger than their similarities.

Dylan guaranteed rock a future in the '60s when he demonstrated that the music was a vital form of artistic expression. Springsteen hasn't revolutionized rock songwriting, yet he has made arguably as vital a contribution to the rock tradition by giving people something and someone to believe in.

It isn't a matter of bigger or best when analyzing Dylan or Springsteen or Presley or Little Richard. Despite the temptation to link artists musically, greatness always asserts its own identity. Dylan did exactly what was necessary in an era when rock's artistry was in question. Springsteen played the same essential role in a time when rock's heart was in doubt.

It was dawn when Springsteen left the studio. While most of the artists who had participated in the session stepped into waiting limousines, Bruce walked through the A&M gates toward his car, which he had parked up the street. When an A&M security guard asked if he wanted an escort, Springsteen just smiled. "No, thanks. I can make it on my own."

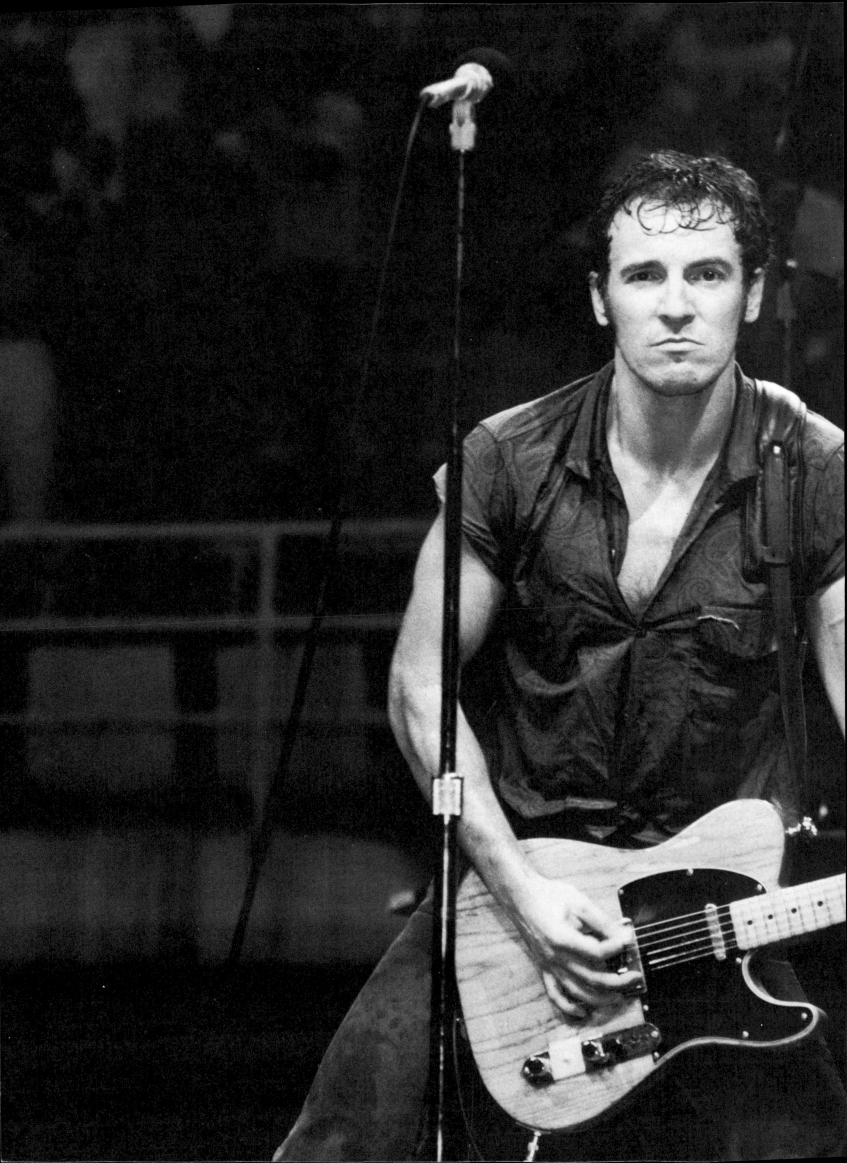

Catholic school girls crowd Bruce's van in Philadelphia, 1984.